LOVE, LONGING & LIFE

CHAITALI KULKARNI

ISBN 979-888569056-0

Dedicated to,

My Beloved Mother

Late Mrs Mangala Shirke

Love You Mom !!!

Contents

Preface

This is my first publication as an author (poet). The journey of life inspired me to write this book. Love is a beautiful feeling which we all experience in every walk of our life. The various emotions of happiness, pain and so on that we experience in this journey of love are what I've tried to put through words in this book.

You might be able to relate some of your love experiences with one or the other poem in this book.

Hope you all enjoy reading it and feel the love.

1. LOVE !!!

LOVE is a feeling which can only be felt,
expressing is just not possible and speaking of is difficult yet
LOVE speaks in its own way,
sometimes it's the eyes else the heartbeats which have all to say
LOVE inspires one to dream, LOVE gives our life a theme
LOVE makes everything possible and can be the only reason for every event
humans, the creatures all would die but LOVE will still remain
the world, the universe all would be destroyed but LOVE will never end
LOVE is the only truth, LOVE is eternal!!!

2. Thoughts

Enter Caption

Several thoughts in my mind,
some were true, I now find,
but some were false, and,
those were your calls,
from far away that I had heard,
but, those were thoughts just to hurt.

3. Thinking of you

*

Whenever, I remember you,
the only thing I do is just close my eyes and see you.
but, it's just for a while, that I see your smile,
for then you go, leaving me alone with your love.
*

Whenever you find yourself to be alone &
need someone to rely on
then my dear if you can,
just turn around and give your hand,
you would find my arms spreaded
to hold on to you as tight as I can.

4. Words unspoken

My dreams are all shattered,
the words left unspoken,
my eyes seem to water,
and the heart is all broken,
to know that I am not the one,
who is your love?
but there is an another person for whom these feelings you have.

5. Desires

This night when from behind the trees,
comes the soothing moonlight,
then there in my eyes, it's your lovable sight
the moon so far in the sky, as you are thy,
I wish, I could get it,
but, Oh! It's a great sigh…

6. Going along with you

My nights have turned brighter,
with your dreams in my eyes
and the days have turned darker,
as for your love my heart cries
Such is the state of my mind,
that I have left myself behind,
just going along with you,
over miles and miles.

7. Hoping you realize...

Meeting you, seeing you is always a desire,
in the depth of my heart which lies,
I wish I could ever see this desire,
in your eyes,
wherein you be eager to meet me,
desperate to be close to me,
you realize the love you have,
and find out ways to express it to me.

8. Trying hard ...

Enter Caption

Trying to live without you but all the efforts in vain,
trying to forget you, but your memories make me go insane
trying to get away from you, but then my feet walk your lane
trying to portray, as to how firm I am,
but then I hear my heart say, how wrong I am
Each and every moment, I tried not to love you,
But, each and every moment I fell more in love with you
Never the colour of my love for you could fade,
but with each and every passing moment, it grew darker in shade.

9. Always

Lost in your thoughts always
always with you each and every moment
my eyes have a sight of you always,
my ears just hear the words you say,
on my lips it's your name always
"I LOVE YOU" is just what my heart says
you and you, just you, always around me
in my thoughts, in my memories, existing in me,
even after my last breath, I'll love you forever the same way
Even after my death, my love for you would live always !!!

10. Play game...

Each & everything around reminds me of you,
I wonder at times whether the same happens with you
but then I tend to forget,
that it was just a game you played,
to win over and gain
whatever you desired to get
Not even for a moment did you repent,
playing with someone's heart, ripping it apart.

11. Broken...

We planned to be one, be together and make life fun,
walk one path and stay in each other's heart
but still, words were left unspoken,
the promises were broken
Finally you went apart and broke my heart
when I was just trying to survive,
you made me die hard.

12. Fear of Losing you

When you are with me, & hold me close in your arms tight
I just feel so free, secured and that everything is just gonna be right,
but as your hands start loosening &
I find myself moving out of your arms,
I start losing faith in myself and everything seems to go dark
the feeling of insecurity takes over me
I find myself lost in a deep sea,

whose waves have grown wild and are drowning me &
I stand helpless with no one around me,
striving hard to survive, with a will to be alive
but then my fate, giving me no time.

13. Reflecting

Today almost after a year, when we have been together,
I just sit back and think over,
as to what went wrong, why we went apart,
after coming so long, why did you break my heart?
If you had to do this, why was that first kiss,
If you had to hurt me so much, why was that first touch
You said you liked a smile on my face,
but instead, you made me cry always
I had my trust in you, but, I never understood,
whether I should, believe your words or in what you do
Tell me how do I forget those moments
when you held me tight in your arms,

and today you have left me all alone to lament,
with just your name written on my palms
Tell me how do I forget you,
when I can feel your existence in me,
and tell me how do I live without you,
when I can feel your soul resting in me.

14. Why...?

Lost in myself, not aware of what's happening around,
I'm all alone although standing in a crowd
There is a smile on my face but my heart is crying aloud,
Why all this mess, what is it all about?
With my eyes closed, I dreamt of being with you forever and ever,

but didn't realize, that when I open my eyes, the dreams will shatter
leaving me into pieces and my eyes to water
I wonder at times, why did we ever meet,
why did we come so close and made memories so sweet
when we had to go different ways, why did we try walking one street
when we had to go apart why did we stay in each other's heart
when we were not to carry on, why did we even make a start.

15. Memories

No moment I'm all alone,
I start with the journey of my memories
Right from the day one, when you took me in your arms and proposed me
or the moment when you forced to get a kiss from me
back to the day when even a moment for you was hard without me, or,
when I heard a say that you could spend your life with me
the day when my eyes met yours
and when I couldn't find a way out of your arms

I remember our love being so true
you loving me and I loving you,
the night we spent looking at the stars,
holding hands trying to read each others heart
Tears rolling down our eyes,
we, beholding each other in our arms tight,
feeling the soul penetrating each others heart,
and at the same time going through the pain of moving apart
Though not for long, that our relationship could last
but our love is so strong,
that it would never be a past.

16. Gone are the days...

Gone are the days, when we loved each other,
found out ways to be together,
days when our eyes met, expressed words unsaid
When I just needed to trust, your touch,
made me believe you loved me so much
But then now I realize, that everything was just lies
when I was in your arms, it was just another chance,
for you to play and then get away
without any repent, pretending to be innocent
I wonder how could you be so mean,
that when I needed you, you were never to be seen,

but, always found me whenever you were keen
I wonder what to believe, the moments we loved each other
or the time when we are strangers
For me, it wouldn't be possible ever again,
to pass through this love lane,
cause it's too difficult to go through the pain,
of being betrayed by the one you love like an insane.

17. Lost Faith

It was just smiles when I was with you,
cause I believed your lies, that you love me too
Dreams and just dreams, that's what you gave me,
but then I forgot, dreams are never to come true
Today it's just these dreams left with me,

as you have left me all alone in this wild love sea
but then still, your loveable memories make me happy
Suddenly the tears in my eyes, make me realize
that you have forgotten everything so easily
To rely on anyone now is difficult somehow
cause trust is something I have lost,
in myself and everyone, I come across.

18. Being Loved...

Never I expected a person would fall in love with me &
when you said those words, "I Love You",
I was surprised, how could this be?
with you in my life, I find myself to be the most lucky,
your love, your gentle touch, makes me aware of my existence,
my beauty,
In your arms when I am cuddled,
I find myself to be on top of the world,
As you kiss me, your love runs through my blood,
So much you have loved me, I find you existing in me,
I have lost my soul to you; it is your soul resting in me.

19. Alive again

As I close my eyes, it's your sight, crisp and clear in my heart
strong and mature, but soft at heart and full of care
Feelings intense, need and want for me, always the same
Blessed I am, with your love, simple and plain
Every moment you make me feel special.
putting me on top of the world
but, I am scared now of falling down from there
it's good to feel special but I hate this feeling of scare
Just be there for me as you have always been,
holding on and clinging on to me
Right now, it's only in words that I can express
so just believe them and understand their essence
As they come straight from the depth of my heart
to tell you, that, I LOVE YOU !!!

20. Becoming ONE

I remember the day we met,
known to each other but unknown yet,
there was something, some love vibe ,
that ran through me as we had our first ride,
the talks we had, the feelings we shared,
the way you held my hand and the way your eyes stared,
they just told me that you were in love with me and you wanted me there,
that's when I knew too, that I was in love with you,
though I tried to leave, I still wanted so much to be held by you and that's what you did,
held me back and didn't let me leave,
your feelings reached my heart through your touch, your words and your stare,

I so much wanted to trust them and be yours that very moment
I'm so glad for that day, cos it got us together forever to stay,
to sail through the ocean beyond the horizon,
and just become "ONE".

Straight From The Heart...

The words in the book come straight from the heart and hence, I hope they reach out to the heart of every reader. The book is a mixed bag of emotions experienced in love...

With this, I hope that my every reader finds their soulmate and they fill each other's life with LOVE, LOVE and Lots of LOVE ...

9 798885 690560

Printed by Libri Plureos GmbH in Hamburg, Germany